Grandad & Nana's House

LET'S COUNT TO TWENTY!!

Yolanda Henderson

Copyright ©2023 by Yolanda Henderson
All rights reserved
Illustrated by Bobooks

Dedication

I dedicate this book to my middle two grandchildren, Lauren Taylor & Caleb. They have brought so much joy & laughter (plenty of laughter) into our lives. I pray they take advantage of ALL that life has to offer and then create what it doesn't!

One sunny Saturday morning, Grandaddy and Nana were sitting outside enjoying a hot cup of coffee. The cheerful sounds of birds chirping and flowers blossoming made their spring time morning even more relaxing.

The phone began to ring.
When grandaddy answered, it was their son Charles.
He was called into work and needed a babysitter
IMMEDIATELY.

Nana had plans to go get her nails done, have brunch with her girlfriends, and do a little shopping. She knew her day had changed from "hanging with the girls" to "hanging with the grands."

About an hour later the doorbell began to ring..... continuously. Grandaddy opens the door and in runs Lauren and Caleb yelling, "hello grandaddy....hello nana, we're here!" Nana greeted them the same yelling, "My Buttercup and Juicy Ju, I'm so happy to see you!" They immediately asked, "what are we going to do today Nana." Caleb and Lauren know that Nana always have activities planned during their visit.

Nana replied "We are going to bake cookies and learn how to count to 20." Lauren and Caleb were so excited they began jumping up and down.

Lauren quickly stopped, put her hands on her hips and said "I don't know how to bake cookies, so I'm gonna learn how to count annnnd bake cookies too." Nana looked at Lauren, smiled, nodded yes, and said "We're going to have lots of fun.

Nana, Lauren, and Caleb were busy mixing ingredients for the cookies. Nana decided they would take turns placing the cookies on the tray. Caleb said "I'm gonna put the FIRST cookie on the tray"

Lauren scooped cookie number

TWO

before she tied her shoe!

Caleb was ready for cookie number

THREE

before Nana could finish
making a pitcher of tea.

Lauren was dropping cookie dough all over the floor before she could get to cookie number **FOUR**.

Caleb thought he was going to need the knives for cookie number

FIVE.

Lauren thought the dough needed to be mixed before she scooped cookie number

SIX!

Nana decided to heat the oven. She knew the house was about to smell like heaven while Caleb sooped cookie number

SEVEN.

Just before Lauren scooped out cookie number
EIGHT,
she and Caleb were having a debate about whose cookie would be great.

Caleb wanted to put a design on cookie number **NINE**.

Caleb and Lauren took a break in the den to chat with grandaddy and that left Nana to scoop out cookie number

TEN.

The oven was heated when it was cookie number seven. It should be ready because Lauren is scooping cookie number **ELEVEN**.

Caleb tried to do it himself by getting another tray off the shelf to put cookie number **TWELVE**.

Lauren was ready to clean after she scooped out cookie number
THIRTEEN!

13

Caleb said Lauren was being mean because she wouldn't help him scoop cookie number **FOURTEEN**.

14

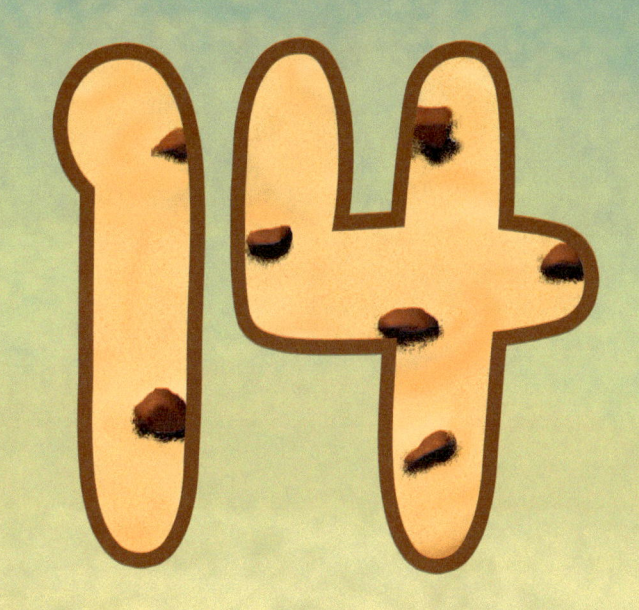

Lauren put on a tiara and called herself a queen before she scooped out cookie number
FIFTEEN.

15

Caleb asked if he could put green on his cookie number **SIXTEEN**.

16

Lauren said her hands were unclean and she needed to wash them before scooping cookie number **SEVENTEEN**.

17

Grandaddy decided to help with cookie number

EIGHTEEN

before he put cloths into the washing machine.

18

Lauren helped Caleb scoop cookie number
NINETEEN
to show him she wasn't mean.

19

Nana scooped cookie number

TWENTY

which made them have plenty.

20

Caleb and Lauren were
so excited to learn how to make cookies and count to
TWENTY. When their dad came to get them, they didn't
leave Grandaddy and Nana with many. As a matter of
fact they took

ALL TWENTY!!

Made in the USA
Columbia, SC
22 June 2024